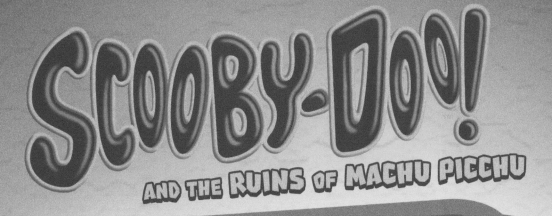

SCOOBY-DOO!
AND THE RUINS OF MACHU PICCHU

THE HIDDEN CITY HOWLER

BY MARK WEAKLAND

Consultant: David Chicoine, PhD
Associate Professor, Department
of Geography and Anthropology
Louisiana State University

CAPSTONE PRESS
a capstone imprint

T0051059

Scooby-Doo and the gang heard about a mystery at the ruins of Machu Picchu in Peru. As they hiked along the Inca Trail, they were ready to start investigating.

"At night the city is filled with howling," explained Carlos, their guide. "Tourists won't visit because they think the place is haunted."

We'll get to the bottom of this mystery.

As they approached the ancient city . . .

This is where I leave you. Good luck.

Carlos turned down the trail and walked out of sight with his llama. A faint howl echoed in the distance.

Zoinks! It sure is spooky out here. Like, look at all this fog!

Don't worry, guys. It's only mist. It forms because Machu Picchu is high up in the tropical mountain forests. The heat, moisture, and high elevation create the mist.

SCOOBY FACT

Machu Picchu is located on a ridge in the Andes Mountain range, almost 8,000 feet (2,438 meters) above sea level. Some visitors suffer from headaches, dizziness, or nausea because of the high elevation.

Fred stopped at an overlook. "There's Machu Picchu! I see lots of places for the howler to hide."

Shaggy looked at the city below. "The howler is down there? Like, maybe we should leave him alone and turn back."

Scooby peeked at the city from behind Shaggy and nodded nervously.

"Come on, guys. We came all this way," said Velma. "Let's start investigating."

SCOOBY FACT

In the 1400s and 1500s, the Incas ruled the western part of South America from Colombia to central Chile.

"The city has more than 200 buildings," said Daphne, reading from her tablet. "They range from small houses to large temples. Machu Picchu was built on levels to fit all of its structures. There are more than 100 flights of stairs!"

"Who built all of this?" asked Fred.

"Archeologists think the city was built by the Incas in 1450," said Daphne.

The gang walked to the entrance of Machu Picchu.

"Like, why would somebody build a city all the way up here?" asked Shaggy, looking around.

"Good question," said Daphne. "Some archaeologists think Machu Picchu was a royal estate for powerful emperors, leaders, and nobles. Others think it was a secret place to hold religious ceremonies. And some think the city was built for both of these reasons."

Shaggy scratched his head. "It sounds like there's a lot to learn about the people who lived here."

Daphne pulled out her tablet and showed the gang what Machu Picchu looked like long ago. "The Incas had many skills. They made beautiful buildings and carved complex designs. They built terraces for growing crops. They even developed special types of corn and potatoes that grew in harsh climates." Velma pointed to the image on Daphne's tablet.

Machu Picchu was divided into separate districts. Each one had a specific purpose. The people who worked in the fields and built houses lived in one district. Farmers grew crops in another. Royalty lived in a third area. There was also a sacred place that contained all of Machu Picchu's religious temples.

"Many of these stones weigh more than 50 tons," said Fred.

"Heavy," said Shaggy. "Like, how did they get here?"

"Some were carved right here. Others came from farther down the mountain," said Fred. "Archeologists believe hundreds of men pushed the stones here. The Incas didn't use wheels."

Daphne ran her hand along the wall. "These buildings were constructed without mortar. The stones are cut so finely that even a knife's blade couldn't fit between them."

As the others walked ahead, Scooby-Doo put his ear on one of the stones. He listened for sounds behind the wall. Suddenly a loud howl filled the air.

Zoinks! Let's get out of here, Scoob.

Shaggy and Scooby caught up with the rest of the gang as they stood in front of a large rectangular stone.

"What is this?" asked Fred, pointing to the stone.

"It's the Intihuatana stone," said Velma. "It was very important to Inca religious ceremonies. The Incas worshipped what they saw in the sky. They believed the sun and stars were gods."

"Archeologists discovered how important the sky was to the Incas after studying the structures at Machu Picchu," said Daphne. She pulled up a painting of an Inca religious ceremony on her tablet. "The Incas could see the sun rise at the Temple of the Three Windows. The Intihuatana stone could have been used to observe the stars."

"The Incas may have also believed that the Intihuatana stone tied the sun to the Earth. The stone kept the sun from flying away," added Velma.

It was night now, and the mist had disappeared. The Milky Way was beginning to glow overhead. Scooby pricked up his ears. He didn't hear anything, but he was still spooked.

"The windows were placed here to keep track of the summer and winter solstices," said Fred.

"Like, how can windows do that?" asked Shaggy, scratching his head.

"There is a stone inside the temple that could have been used as an altar," explained Fred. "During the June solstice, the sun's rays would shine directly into one of the temple's windows. The light would connect the window to the stone."

"The Incas had no electricity to light the long nights. Crops did not grow well in winter," said Velma. "The Incas would use the temple to tell them when it would start to get lighter and warmer outside."

SCOOBY FACT

In the northern hemisphere, the summer solstice is in June. It is the longest day of the year. The winter solstice is the shortest day of the year. It occurs in December. Machu Picchu is in the southern hemisphere. Here, the summer solstice is in December and the winter solstice is in June.

"Why was the city abandoned?" asked Fred.

"In the 1500s the Inca Empire was conquered by Spanish invaders called conquistadores," said Daphne. "The conquistadores destroyed almost every Inca city, but Machu Picchu was hidden high in the mountains. It wasn't destroyed because the invaders didn't know it was there."

"Then why don't people still live here?" asked Shaggy.

"One reason is that the Spanish settlers brought diseases with them," said Velma. "The Incas grew sick and died from illnesses, such as smallpox. The city was eventually abandoned and forgotten."

A gust of wind ruffled Daphne's hair. A long, low howl rolled through the air. Shaggy shuddered. "I sure hope the Incas aren't haunting this place!"

"If the city was hidden so well that conquistadores couldn't find it, how was Machu Picchu finally discovered?" asked Fred.

"By an American historian named Hiram Bingham," said Daphne, clicking on Bingham's photo. "Bingham arrived in Peru in 1911. A farmer told him about a ruined city at the top of a nearby mountain."

"Machu Picchu!" said Fred.

"Right, Fred," said Daphne. "Bingham climbed the mountain and met a group of local people. An 11-year-old boy stepped forward to be his guide. The boy led Bingham to Machu Picchu."

"Bingham wrote about his discovery in a book called *The Lost City of the Incas*," Velma added. "People who read the book flocked to Peru. They were eager to see the mysterious city for themselves."

Scooby's ears twitched as the gang investigated the highest part of the city.

"This is the Main, or Principal, Temple of Machu Picchu," said Fred. "Over there is a carved stone altar. Do you see those rectangular cavities? There are seventeen of them. Some believe they were used for burials."

Another gust of wind rushed through the temple, blowing in and out of the cavities. The howling was suddenly all around them.

"Oh, no! It's the howler!" yelled Shaggy.

Fred aimed his flashlight at the stones. The wind blew again and a long, low moan poured from the wall.

"The sound is coming from the cavities," said Fred.

"You're right, Fred," said Velma. "The cavities are *making* the sounds. When the sun sets, the wind picks up. The howling noise is the wind whooshing through the cavities in the temple."

"Like when you blow across the top of a bottle," said Shaggy.

"Correct," said Fred. "Well that solves the mystery of the hidden city howler."

There may not be any ghosts here, but the Inca spirit is still in Machu Picchu.

SCOOBY SNACK-SIZED FACTS

- At the height of its power, the Inca Empire had a population of more than 12 million people.

- The Inca Trail leads to Machu Picchu. Every year tourists hike for days along this ancient road to reach the city.

- Machu Picchu means "Old Peak" in Quechua, the language used by the Incas.

- Machu Picchu is Peru's most famous archeological site. To keep it from being overrun by tourists, the Peruvian government limits the number of visitors per day.

- When Hiram Bingham discovered Machu Picchu, he thought it was another lost Inca city called Vilcabamba. The real Vilcabamba was discovered in 1964.

GLOSSARY

altar (AWL-tur)—a large table in a house of worship, used for religious ceremonies

ancient (AYN-shunt)—from a long time ago

archeologist (ar-kee-AH-luh-jist)—a scientist who learns about people in the past by digging up old buildings and objects and carefully examining them

cavity (KAV-uh-tee)—a hole or hollow space in something solid

conquistador (kon-KEYS-tuh-dor)—a military leader in the Spanish conquest of North and South America during the 1500s

estate (e-STAYT)—a large piece of land, usually with a house on it

hemisphere (HEM-uhss-fihr)—one half of the earth

mortar (MOR-tur)—a mixture of lime, sand, water, and cement that is used for building

sacred (SAY-krid)—holy, or having to do with religion

smallpox (SMAWL-poks)—a disease that spreads easily from person to person, causing chills, fevers, and blisters that scar

solstice (SOL-stiss)—the days of the year when the sun rises at its most northern and southern points

terrace (TER-iss)—a raised, flat platform of land with sloping sides

READ MORE

Barber, Nicola. *Lost Cities.* Treasure Hunters. Chicago: Capstone Raintree, 2013.

Garbe, Suzanne. *Secrets of Machu Picchu: Lost City of the Incas.* Archeological Mysteries. North Mankato, Minn.: Capstone Press, 2015.

Raum, Elizabeth. *Machu Picchu.* Ancient Wonders. Mankato, Minn.: Amicus High Interest, 2015.

INTERNET SITES

Use FactHound to find Internet sites related to this book.

Visit *www.facthound.com*

Just type in 9781515775140 and go.

Super-cool stuff!

Check out projects, games and lots more at
www.capstonekids.com

INDEX

Published in 2018 by Capstone Press, a Capstone Imprint
1710 Roe Crest Drive
North Mankato, Minnesota 56003
www.mycapstone.com

Library of Congress Cataloging-in-Publication Data
Names: Weakland, Mark, author.
Title: Scooby Doo! and the ruins of Machu Picchu : the hidden city howler / by Mark Weakland.
Description: North Mankato, Minn. : Capstone Press, 2018. | Series: Scooby-doo!. Unearthing ancient civilizations with Scooby-Doo!

Identifiers: LCCN 2017034025 (print) | LCCN 2017035444 (ebook) | ISBN 9781515775225 (eBook PDF) | ISBN 9781515775140 (library binding) | ISBN 9781515775188 (paperback)
Subjects: LCSH: Machu Picchu Site (Peru)—Juvenile literature. | Incas—Juvenile literature.
Classification: LCC F3429.1.M3 (ebook) | LCC F3429.1.M3 W43 2018 (print) |
DDC 985/.019—dc23
LC record available at https://lccn.loc.gov/2017034025

Editorial Credits:
Editor: Michelle Hasselius
Designer: Ted Williams
Art Director: Nathan Gassman
Production Specialist: Laura Manthe

Design Elements:
Shutterstock: natashasha

The illustrations in this book were created traditionally, with digital coloring.

TITLES IN THIS SET

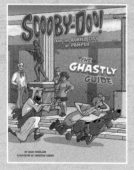